Welcome to Outer Space, Earthling!

This pack offers a collection of fun activities for young children to accompany any study of space and the solar system.

The activities are highly practical, involving hands-on exploration, encouraging discovery techniques, design and making skills and individual creativity.

The activities are cross-curricular and introduce the highly complex study of space through simple child-centred starting points. At the base of each page, there is a list of skills, tequniques, concepts and curriculum areas covered.

For ease of planning, each activity lists resources required, adult-led introductions, pupil activities, useful questions to ask, extension activities for further study and important vocabulary.

The activities provide a perfect companion to the multi-sensory approach to learning that storysacks encourage.

Have fun!

Contents:

Sucked into Space!.. 4
Terrific Telescopes!... 8
Space Sequencing!... 11
Space Spinners!... 12
Space Symmetry!... 16
Bouncing Space Balls and Let's get Fruity!........ 21
Space Snacks!.. 22
The Aliens came two by two!................................. 24
Space in a Box!... 27
Space Jigsaws!.. 28
Postcards from Space!.. 32
Twinkle, twinkle!... 37
Funny Faces from Space!...................................... 38
Let's Make Planets!... 42
Little Moon's Special Mission Patch!................... 44
Astronaut's Alphabet!.. 48
Hands Across the Universe!.................................. 50
Solar Sandwiches!.. 54
Little Moon's Word Search!.................................... 56

Sucked into Space!

Preparation and Resources:

Photocopy Activity Sheet No 1 – enough for one per child.
Show the children the picture of a black hole in the storybook.
Gather together a collection of stoppers that suck or stick to walls e.g. sink plunger, rubber stoppers that hold things in kitchens, etc.

Borrow a vacuum cleaner from the caretaker.
You will need a glass or plastic see-through jug, water, food colouring or ink.

You will also need access to a sink, bath or shower base.
Finally, you will need washing-up bowls one per group of six and something to stir water with.
It would be fun to end the session with each child sucking a sweet or a lolly. (Be aware of safety and food allergies.)

Opener:

Arrive in the classroom sucking a lolly.
Make lots of noise!
Try and talk with the lolly in your mouth, then take it out and apologise for your poor manners.
Focus on the word "suck".
Talk about thumb sucking.

forces • investigation • suction • black holes

Useful questions to ask:

Why do we suck our thumbs?
What other things do we suck? e.g. sweets, ice-lolly, jelly.

Begin to vacuum the classroom, singing as you clean.

Talk about how a vacuum sucks up dirt and dust.
Let the children feel the power of the suck on the end of the extension with their hand.
Talk about an elephant's trunk.

Look at the picture of the black hole in the "Little Moon" storybook. Talk about how it pulls and sucks everything in its way like a giant plug hole in space.

Fill a jug with water and stir it very fast. Drop a tiny drip of ink into the water and let the children see it swirl to the bottom.
Show them the same in a sink.

Activities:

Let the children have fun swirling ink or food colouring into swirling water in washing-up bowls or a water tray.
Let them have fun sticking stoppers and plungers onto wet surfaces.

Extension:

Make hanging black hole swirls using Activity Sheet No 1.
Have a 'sucking race'. The children are given a straw and a grape. They have to suck the grape onto the end of the straw and race across the hall!

Vocabulary:

suck, plunger, stick, twirl, swirl, stir, vacuum, black hole

forces • investigation • suction • black holes

ACTIVITY SHEET NO 1

Step one:
cut along the white line carefully

forces • investigation • suction • black holes

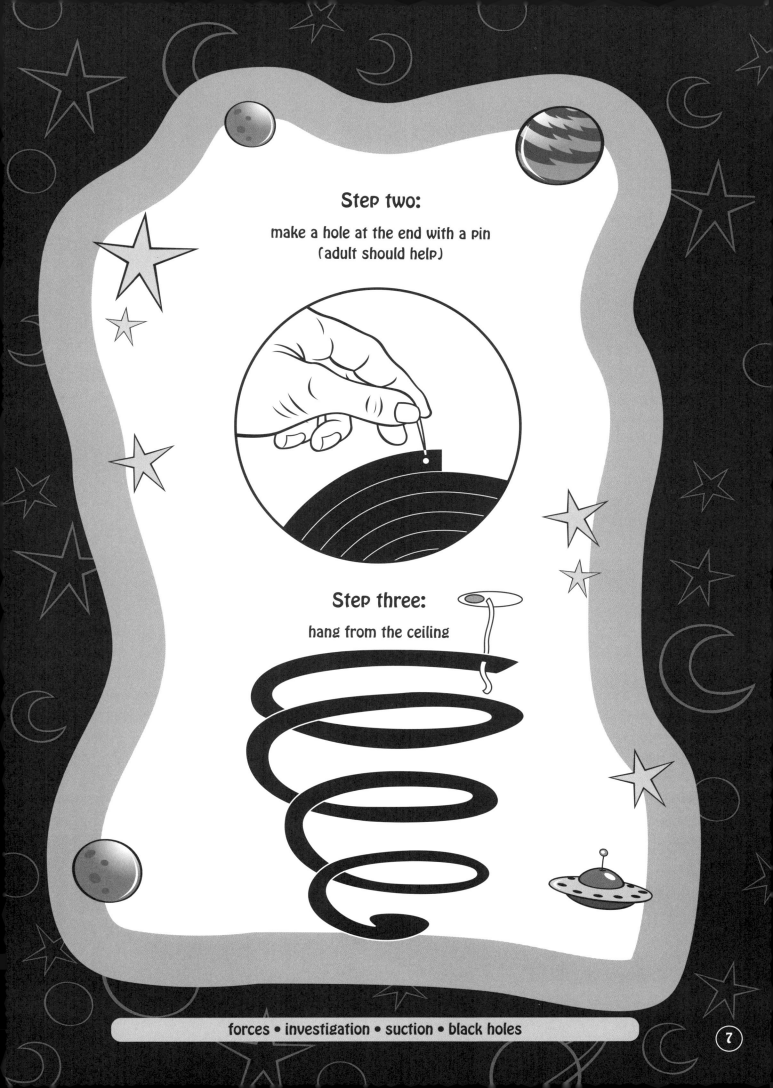

Step two:
make a hole at the end with a pin (adult should help)

Step three:
hang from the ceiling

forces • investigation • suction • black holes

Terrific Telescopes!

Preparation and Resources:

Gather a collection of items that magnify e.g. magnifying glass, spectacles, camera with lens, binoculars, microscope and a telescope if possible. It would really help the children observe magnification if an overhead projector was available. Objects can then be placed on it and magnified. Ask the children to bring in cardboard tubes from home to make their telescope. A variety of sizes are needed. Make view finders like this for the children to look through before the lesson.

You will need:
paint, felt pens, paper, glue, a stapler, crayons, pencils.
Photocopy Activity Sheet No 2 – enough for children to use them as a reference.

Opener:

Walk around the classroom with a magnifying glass, as if you are a detective.
Let children pretend too.
Bring the children to the carpet.
Explore the collection of magnifiers.
Talk about magnification.

magnification • design & make • art • observation • telescopes

Useful questions to ask:

Why do we need to see things more closely and larger then life?
Who needs magnification?
How does magnification help us?

Let the children enjoy using the binoculars, magnifying glasses, overhead projector, microscope, cameras, etc. in and around the school.

You might go on a:
- 'magnification' walk.
- spy mission looking for evidence.
- photo-shoot.
- bird watch.

To give the children a sense of looking through a telescope, let them look through the tiny hole viewers at the world around them.

Activity:

Whilst the telescopes they will make will be for fun and not magnification, the children will greatly enjoy designing the latest in telescope 'fashions'.

The children can create extra long telescopes using three or four tubes.

If tubes of different dimensions cannot be found, simply roll card and staple to the appropriate size.

magnification • design & make • art • observation • telescopes

ACTIVITY SHEET NO 2

Activity Sheet No 2 will be useful for ideas for further designs.

Extensions:

Go on a bug hunt with a magnifying glass.
Put finger prints on paper with ink and look at them under a magnifying glass.

Vocabulary:

enlarge, magnify, blow-up, view, lens, focus, close-up, spectacles, binoculars, microscope, telescopic, telescope

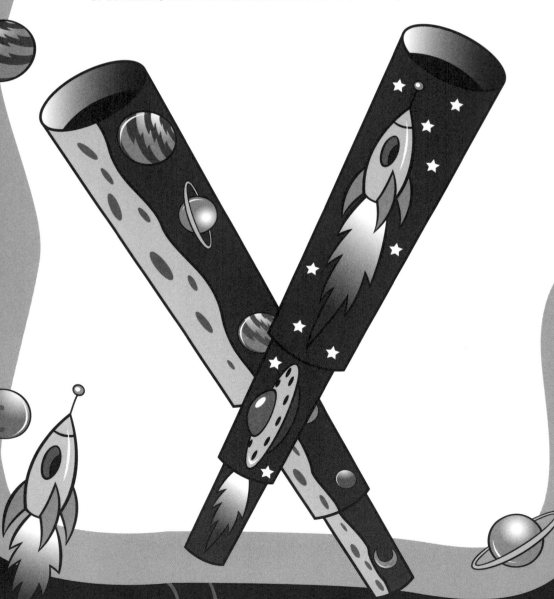

magnification • design & make • art • observation • telescopes

Space Sequencing!

The following pictures are from the "Little Moon" story.
They may be used for a variety of activities:
- sequencing the story
- talking points
- if several copies are made they can be used for a pairs or snap game.
- story mapping

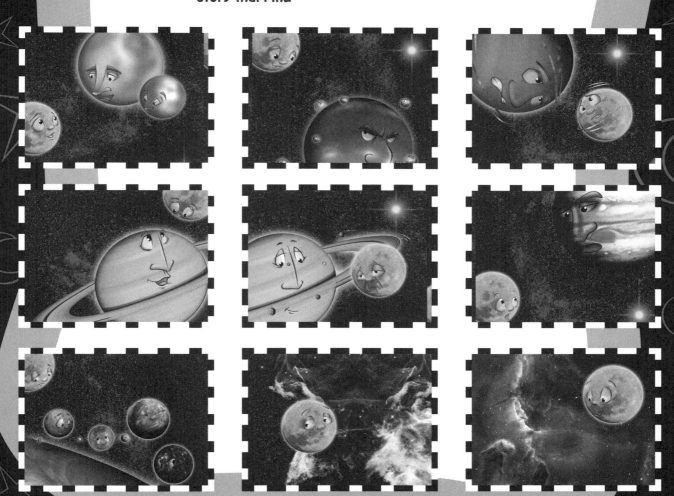

sequencing • story mapping • pairs • memory • discussion

Space Spinners!

Preparation and Resources:

Gather together a collection of objects that spin e.g: balls, spinning tops, coins, jacks, a fishing reel, an electric fan, a knife that spins.

Photocopy Activity Sheet No 3 – enough for each child to have a spinner.

You will need card, scissors, a pin to make a hole in the centre of the spinner, matchsticks that have already been burnt, wool, crayons, plastic hoola hoops, if you have any, and five colours of chiffon-type fabric.

Opener:

Take the children into the playground or hall. Ask the children to hold hands in pairs and carefully dance around and around. Be aware of speed, but they need to feel a little dizzy. Draw circles or create them with skipping ropes. Let the children dance round and round.

If you have mats, the children can pretend to be ice-skaters spinning on the spot. Again take care! Use the fabric to dance and twirl with.
Return to the classroom.
Explore the objects you have collected that spin.
It can be fun for children to feel the air on their faces from a spinning electric fan.
Use the knife and play 'point at me'.

---

rotation • colour mixing • design & make • movement & dance

The children sit in a circle. Someone spins the knife, which is in the middle on a hard surface. If it points at someone, that child is out or must do a 'fun forfeit'.
Finally use balls to show how the planets spin themselves and also spin around the sun as they spin.
This activity could be linked to the 'Bouncing Space Balls' and 'Let's get Fruity'.

Useful questions to ask:

Can you think of things that spin?
What happens to us when we spin?

Activity:

The children can make a spinning top planet or a planet spinner.

Each planet should first be coloured.
Next the child or adult cuts them out.
The planet should then be mounted on card and this should be cut out.
Make holes, using a pin – for a spinning top, one hole; for a spinner, two holes.

To make a spinning top, push a pencil gently into the hole. Be careful to make a small hole, or the top will not spin.

rotation • colour mixing • design & make • movement & dance

To make a spinner, thread wool through the two holes.
Twist the thread and pull.

Have fun!

Extension:

Watch colours blend by creating spinners like this:

Y	B
B	Y

R	Y
Y	R

Vocabulary:

spin, rotate, dizzy, circle

rotation • colour mixing • design & make • movement & dance

ACTIVITY SHEET NO 3

rotation • colour mixing • design & make • movement & dance

Space Symmetry!

Preparation and Resources:

You will need black sugar paper, ready mix paint, brushes, pencils, crayons.

Photocopy Activity Sheet No 4 and cut out enough of the shapes for the whole class to enjoy folding.

Collect symmetrical objects or pictures e.g. butterfly, reading glasses, vase.

You will also need towels, flannels and other items you can fold exactly in half.

Opener:

Tell the children you are in a 'folding' mood! You just can't help folding things today!

Tell them you are so busy folding they will just have to wait. Accidently knock all your folding on the floor. Can they help fold them again?

As they are such good 'folders', could they fold paper shapes too? Give them the moons, stars and planets to fold.
Look at the folding lines down the middle of each shape.

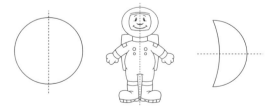

Talk about 'folding in half'. The comet will not fold in half. Explore why.

symmetry • art • design & make • folding in half

Useful questions to ask:

What does it mean to fold?
How do we know we have folded in half?
What do you notice about each half?
Why can't we fold the star in half?

Explore the symmetrical objects and show the 'imaginary line' down the centre.
Talk about the words 'symmetry' and 'symmetrical'.

Activity

Create a symmetrical universe painting.

Step 1: Fold a sheet of black sugar paper in half.

Step 2: With plenty of thick ready mix paint, paint a planet or planets on one half.

Step 3: Quickly, before the planet is able to dry, flick lots of different colours on one half. It will help if you cover the other half with newspaper to protect it.

Step 4: Remove the newspaper, fold the pages in half, press down gently and smooth.

Step 5: Open the paper carefully and you will have a beautiful outer space universe.

If you use glitter paints as well as ready mix paint, your universe will sparkle.

symmetry • art • design & make • folding in half

ACTIVITY SHEET NO 4

Extension:

Photocopy Activity Sheet Nos 4, 5 and 6.
Let the children create their own symmetrical alien and rocket.

Vocabulary:

fold, symmetry, symmetrical, line of symmetry, same, exactly, half

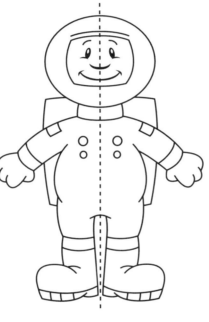

symmetry • art • design & make • folding in half

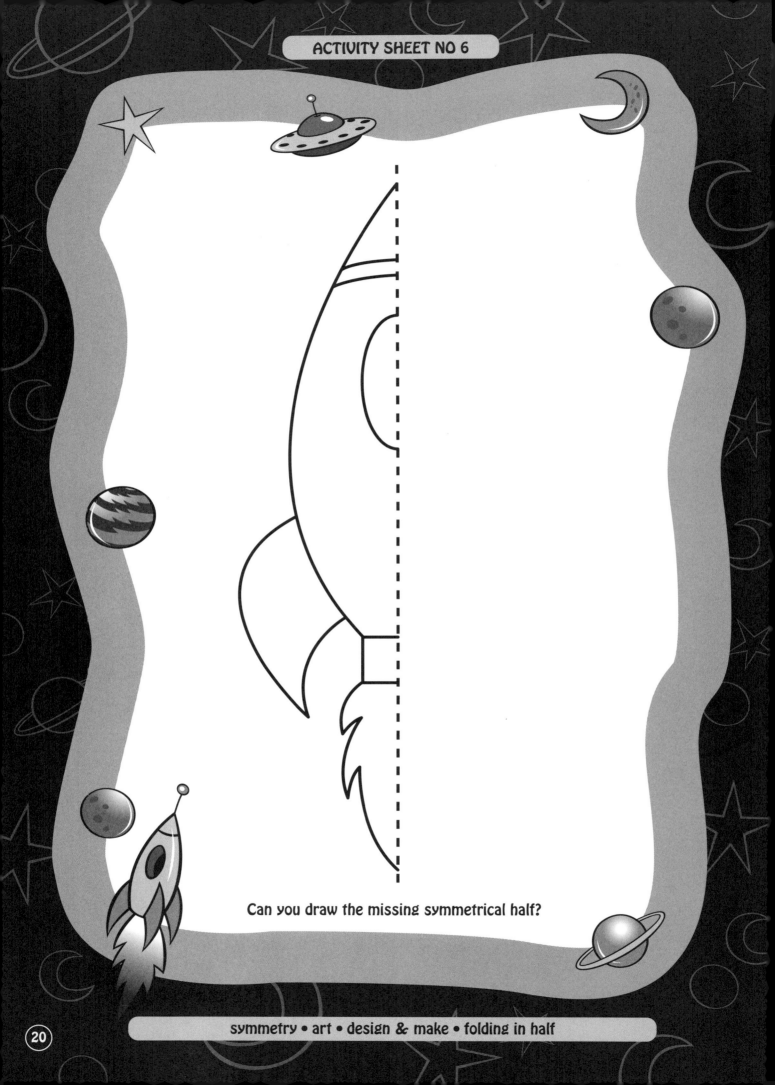

Bouncing Space Balls
and Let's get Fruity!

It can be difficult for children to understand the movements of the planets and their rotation around the sun.

A wonderful way to demonstrate this is to use balls of different sizes.

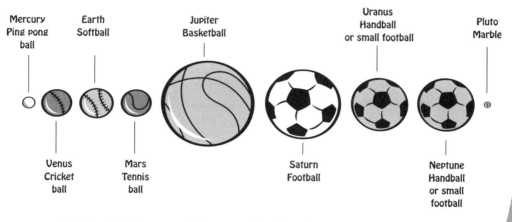

| Mercury – Ping pong ball | Venus – Cricket ball | Earth – Softball | Mars – Tennis ball | Jupiter – Basketball | Saturn – Football | Uranus – Handball or small football | Neptune – Handball or small football | Pluto – Marble |

Whilst it is impossible to make the planets relative in size (1,300 earths could be crammed into Jupiter), it will give the children a sense of how our solar system moves.

Fruits can also be used.

movement • relative size • rotation • our solar system

Space Snacks!

Every class will enjoy a 'space feast' and it can be great fun making unusual food.

The feast might take on a theme e.g. 'Alien Tea', 'Astronaut Supplies', 'Moon Cooking', etc.
As most of the food eaten in space by astronaut is pre-cooked and pre-prepared, the children might explore pre-prepared foods we eat on earth.
Fun can be had changing the colours of food by using edible food colouring.

The following are a range of ideas for things the children might enjoy creating.

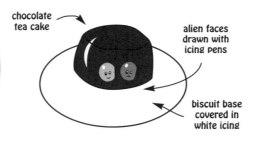

Flying Saucer
- chocolate tea cake
- alien faces drawn with icing pens
- biscuit base covered in white icing

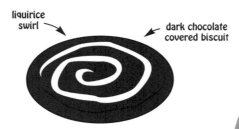

Black hole
- liquirice swirl
- dark chocolate covered biscuit

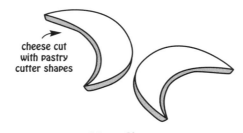

Moon Cheeses
- cheese cut with pastry cutter shapes

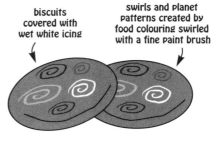

Planet Biscuits
- biscuits covered with wet white icing
- swirls and planet patterns created by food colouring swirled with a fine paint brush

food technology • design & make • hygiene

The Aliens came two by two!

Preparation and Resources:

Gather together a small collection of socks and items that come in pairs e.g. salt and pepper pots, knife and forks, shoes, gloves, bat and ball, pen and paper, etc.
Put on odd socks, gloves or shoes before the lesson begins.
Photocopy Activity Sheet No 7 – one per four children.
Fill a basket with pairs of plastic animals, cars, socks or real fruit pears.
Find a copy of "Alfie's Feet" by Shirley Hughes.

Opener:

See if the children notice your 'odd' clothes without saying anything. Then ask the children to look at you closely. What do they notice?
Tip out the socks and ask the class to help you 'sort' them into pairs, so you can choose a 'matching pair' to wear.
Put a new pair on.
Have fun sorting other collections into pairs.
Read "Alfie's Feet" by Shirley Hughes.
Finally ask the children to take off their shoes and muddle them up into one pile. They will have great fun trying to find them and put them on as quickly as possible!

Useful questions to ask:

Which matches this one?
What does 'identical' mean?
Can you find any pairs?

pairs • memory • matching

Activity

More able pupils may be able to cut up their photocopied activity sheet No 7. Others will need it cut up for them.
Place the class in groups of four.

Game 1: The Memory Game

- Lay the picture-cards face down on a flat surface. Gently mix them around so they are well 'shuffled'.
- Each person takes a turn to turn over any two cards. If the pictures are a match/a pair, that person collects them.
  If they are not a pair, they must be turned over again and left in exactly the same place.

The trick is to watch very carefully and remember where each picture is. Then when your turn comes around, you know exactly where the matching cards are.

The winner is the person with the most pairs after all the cards have been picked up.

Game 2: Snap!

- You can also use the picture cards to play 'snap'.

Extension:

Place the children in pairs. One child draws a space picture on a small, square piece of paper. You might suggest a theme e.g. planets, rockets, etc.

Their partner must then try and copy it as carefully as possible on another square to create a matching pair.

The pairs the class produce can then be used for The Memory Game.

Vocabulary:

pairs, match, twos, odd one out, copy, same, identical

pairs • memory • matching

ACTIVITY SHEET NO 7

Cut out each picture carefully.

pairs • memory • matching

Space in a Box!

Cut a hole in the lid to let light in.

Cut out a small hole to view through.

The children will have great fun creating this scene from space in a box.

If glitter and fluorescent paints are used, the effect is even more dazzling.

art • design & make • landscapes

Space Jigsaws!

Preparation and Resources:

Photocopy and cut up the space picture below. Photocopy Activity Sheet Nos 8 and 9 for each child. You will need a collection of plastic 2D shapes and a stop watch.

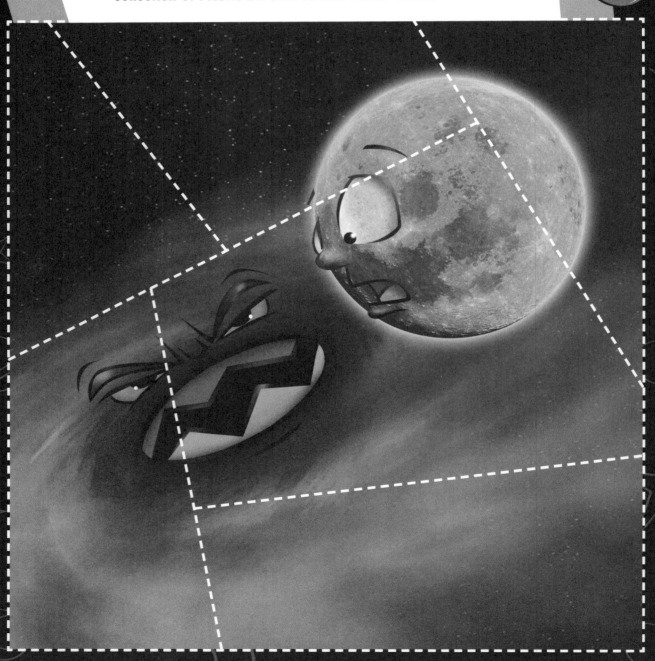

fine motor skills • spatial awareness

Opener:

Take the children for an environmental walk to explore how shapes fit together. Look at: floor tiles, brick patterns, pavings, roof tiles, etc.

On returning to the classroom, lay out the set of plastic shapes on the floor and let the children experiment with fitting shapes together.

Hold up the complete space picture from the previous page.

Choose a pair of children. Give them the same space picture cut into five pieces. Have a 'time challenge' to see how long it takes to re-arrange them into a complete picture. Let another pair attempt to better the time.

Useful questions to ask:

Which shapes fit together like a jigsaw?
Which shapes have round edges?
Which shapes have straight edges?
Which shapes have corners?
Why don't round shapes fit together?
Can any round shapes fit together with straight-edged shapes?
How could round shapes fit together?

Activity:

Give children individually or in pairs the two jigsaws on Activity Sheet Nos 8 and 9.
For more able pupils, these will not be ready-cut. For less able pupils, provide them ready-cut. Let them enjoy assembling the jigsaw.

fine motor skills • spatial awareness

ACTIVITY SHEET NO 8

Extension:

Give the children a collection of pictures from magazines, etc. Let them create their own jigsaw by cutting them into five or six shapes.

They can challenge a friend to fit it together.

Vocabulary:

fit, join, round, straight, edge, tessellate, gaps, cover, jigsaw

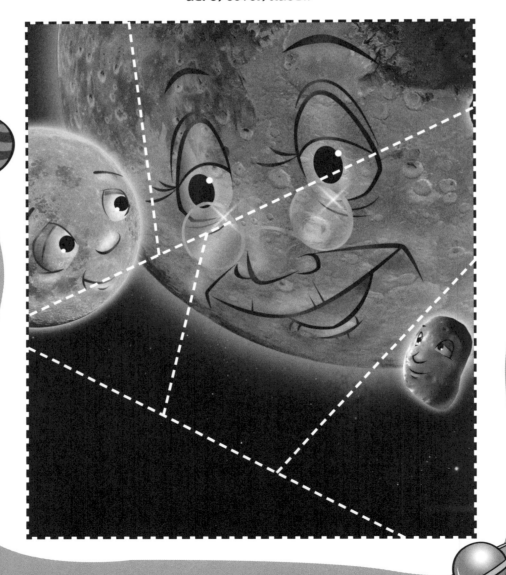

fine motor skills • spatial awareness

Postcards from Space!

Preparation and Resources:

Send the class a postcard through the post.
Gather together a collection of postcards.
Ask the children to bring in postcards from home.
Hang up the "Little Moon" fabric background.
You will also need: "Little Moon" storybook, some other space non-fiction books, crayons and pencils.
Photocopy Activity Sheet Nos 10 and 11 for each child.

Opener:

Ask the school administrator to rush in excitedly with the 'class postcard'.
Gather the class together and read the card.
Talk about: pictures, addresses, stamps, letter section beginning with 'dear ...' and ending 'love ...'
Look at other postcards.
Enjoy sorting by country or day and night pictures, etc.

Useful questions to ask:

Why do we send postcards?
Have you ever sent a postcard? Who to? Where from?
When do we usually send postcards?
Who has sent postcards to you?
Did you like receiving a card? Why?
Why do postcards have pictures or photographs on one side?

writing • art • design

Talk about what to write on postcards:
- how you feel
- what you are doing
- what the weather is
- where you have been
- what it is like where you are staying

Finally, explore the different planets on the 'Little Moon' fabric background. Look at colours, shapes, sizes, patterns.
Find matching pictures in the non-fiction books.

Activity:

Let the children choose a planet to send a postcard from.
Look closely together at the planet of their choice.
Look at colours, patterns, shades and shapes.
Using Activity Sheet Nos 10 and 11, the children make their own postcard design.
They might add: aliens, space-craft, stars, astronauts or even create an imaginary place on the planet surface, e.g. playground, park, zoo, homes, etc.

Finally, the children can create their own simple message on the reverse of the postcard in their own emergent or formal writing. If appropriate to their age and stage of development, they might also write a 'space address'.

Extension Activity:

Photocopy Activity Sheet No 12.
Gather together a collection of stamps.
Design and create your own 'Mars' stamp.

Vocabulary:

postcard, address, alien, astronaut, postage stamp, dear, planet, photograph, love, best wishes, space craft

writing • art • design

ACTIVITY SHEET NO 10

Fold

writing • art • design

ACTIVITY SHEET NO 11

Fold

Wish you were here!

writing • art • design

ACTIVITY SHEET NO 12

writing • art • design

Twinkle, twinkle!

Create your own twinkling night sky!

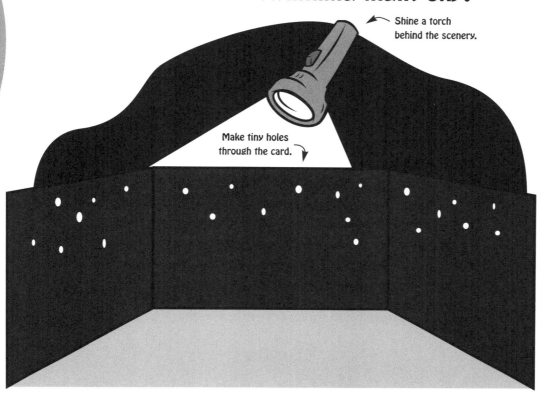

Shine a torch behind the scenery.

Make tiny holes through the card.

You might like to create star constellations with the holes made in the shape of well-known star patterns.

The light should be off and curtains should be drawn for best effect.
(Adult supervision required with pins and scissors).

light sources • star constellations • art • design & make

Funny Faces from Space!

Creating planet people!

Preparation and Resources:

Photocopy Activity Sheet No 13 – enough for one sheet per pair of children.

Cut out enough black and white card or paper circles for the class to have four or five each.

Enlarge to A3 one copy of Activity Sheet No 13. It should be displayed for the class to see at the beginning of the lesson. You will also need five oranges or grapefruits, A4 white paper, felt tips, crayons, chalks, scissors and "Little Moon" book and fabric wall hanging.

Draw a large circle on three separate flip-chart sheets.

Opener:

As the children settle for the beginning of the lesson, make funny faces at them!

Ask them to make the funniest face they can.

Talk about face parts: nose, eye, ears, hair, eye-brows, eye-lashes, lips, teeth, forehead, tongue, cheeks, chins, moustache, beard, side-burns.

Sing the song 'knees and toes' but sing these words:

'lips, eyes, teeth and tongue   or   'chin, cheeks, nose and hair
teeth and tongue.'   nose and hair.'

art • characterisation • design & make • singing

Look closely at the faces on the planets in the "Little Moon" book.
Talk about expressions: sad, happy, cross, sleepy, bored, surprised, afraid, shy, etc.

Ask the children to make different faces to show different moods. They can make a face and the class can guess their mood.

Using the flip-chart, draw a face on one of the circles using very simple lines as used in the "Little Moon" book. This could also be done with chalk on a blackboard or on a white board.
Look closely at the A3 copy of Activity Sheet No 13 displayed. Talk about the different faces. Ask individual children to make a face on the board or flip-chart.
Finally, have fun with the children drawing a face on the oranges and grapefruits.
If ink remains on the wax surface, it can be wiped off with tissue and the fruit used again. However, a permanent marker may be needed.

Useful questions to ask:

What different faces can you make?
What face am I making?
How do you know what I'm feeling by looking at my face?
How does my face tell you what I'm feeling?

art • characterisation • design & make • singing

Activity:

Let the children practise making simple line faces on A4 paper. They should be encouraged to look closely at Activity Sheet No 13 for help.

When they are happy with a face, it can be copied onto a card or paper circle using chalks on black paper or feltpens on white paper.

If both sides are given faces, a wonderful mobile can be created.

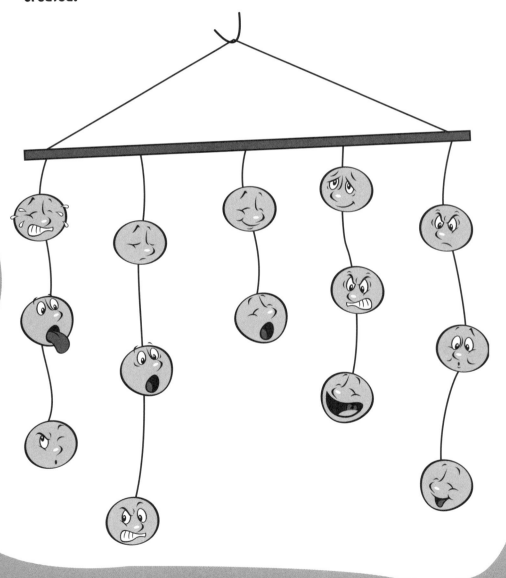

art • characterisation • design & make • singing

ACTIVITY SHEET NO 13

Extension:

Draw faces on the playground with chalks, or paint them with water and a brush and watch them disappear.

Vocabulary:

feeling, mood, expression, face, funny

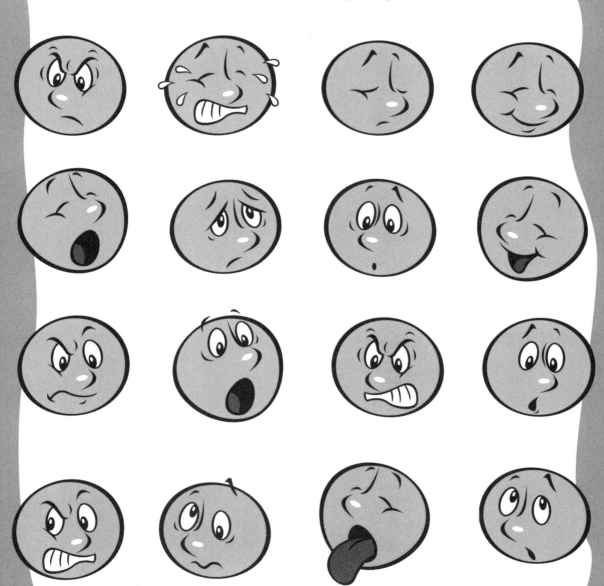

art • characterisation • design & make • singing

Let's Make Planets!

If the children look closely at the photographs in the "Little Moon" storybook and the non-fiction book, they will marvel at the intensity of colour and variety of pattern. The following are a variety of ways the children might create their own wonderful solar system.

Galaxy
created by flicking paint and glitter on a black background with brushes.

absorbent paper similar to ink blotting paper

Swirling planet
created by wetting paper heavily first and then dropping ink or water colour paint on the paper and swirling with fine brush.

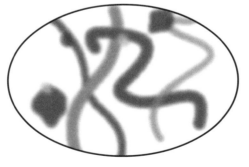

Pastel planet
made by applying pastel crayons and smearing with fingers.

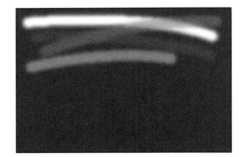

Nebula
created by lightly rubbing chalk or pastels on black paper.

shape • colour • pattern • art • design & make

Marbled planet
made by applying paper to marbling inks

Collage sun
made by sticking shiny paper and bright fabric in golds, reds, yellows and oranges

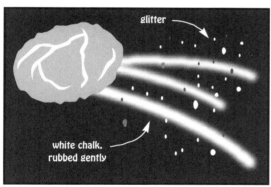

glitter

white chalk, rubbed gently

Sparkling comet
silver foil, glitter, white chalk rubbed gently

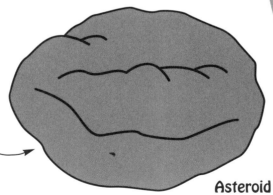

thick paint applied over a thin layer of plaster of paris

Asteroid
thick paint applied over a thin layer of plaster

shape • colour • pattern • art • design & make

Little Moon's Special Mission Patch!

Preparation and Resources:

Gather together a collection of badges from home. Ask any children who are Cubs or Brownies to bring in the sweatshirts to show their badges.

Photocopy Activity Sheet Nos 14 and 15 – enough for one per child.

You will need crayons, feltpens, paints, pencils, collage material, glue, scissors and a copy of the "Little Moon" story. Write a list of the places Little Moon visited and who he met on the black or white board.

Opener:

Wear a badge and see if the children notice it.
Read the story of "Little Moon".
Talk about his mission to find a new home, the places he visited and the planets he met.

Explain the words badge, emblem, patch, logo, etc.
Look at the school emblem.
Examine the children's collection of badges.
Have a Brownie and Cub badge fashion parade.
Look closely at the designs.

art • design & make

Draw a design on the black or white board or flip chart that is cluttered and confusing.

Look at the simplicity of many designs.

Useful questions to ask:
Why do we have badges?
What do badges or patches show us?
When do we wear badges?
What should a badge tell us?

Activity:

Provide each child with a template shape (Activity Sheet Nos 14 and 15) of their choice.
Encourage the children to plan their design on scrap paper. Set them the challenge of creating a "Little Moon" mission patch, using crayons, felt, collage, etc.

Extension:

Create a whole class giant mission patch using collage materials.

Vocabulary

patch, mission, logo, design, emblems, badge, simple

art • design & make

ACTIVITY SHEET NO 14

Just like spacecraft, Little Moon had his own special journey to make. His mission was to find a new home. Design a mission patch for Little Moon. Your design should show something of the journey.
Use your crayons, paints or pastels to make it very special. You could even use collage or mosaic design.

art • design & make

ACTIVITY SHEET NO 15

Just like spacecraft, Little Moon had his own special journey to make. His mission was to find a new home.

Use your crayons, paints or pastels to make it very special. You could even use collage or mosaic design.

art • design & make

Astronaut's Alphabet!

This following alphabet can be photocopied and used for a variety of activities.
1 colouring
2 sequencing activities when cut up
3 two alphabets for matching, memory and snap games when photo-copied and cut up
4 stimulus for talking
5 fun learning the astronaut alphabet

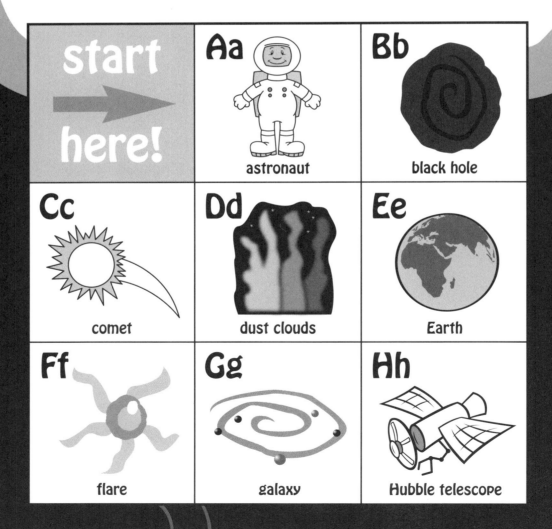

start here!	**Aa** astronaut	**Bb** black hole
Cc comet	**Dd** dust clouds	**Ee** Earth
Ff flare	**Gg** galaxy	**Hh** Hubble telescope

letter regognition • alphabet • sequencing

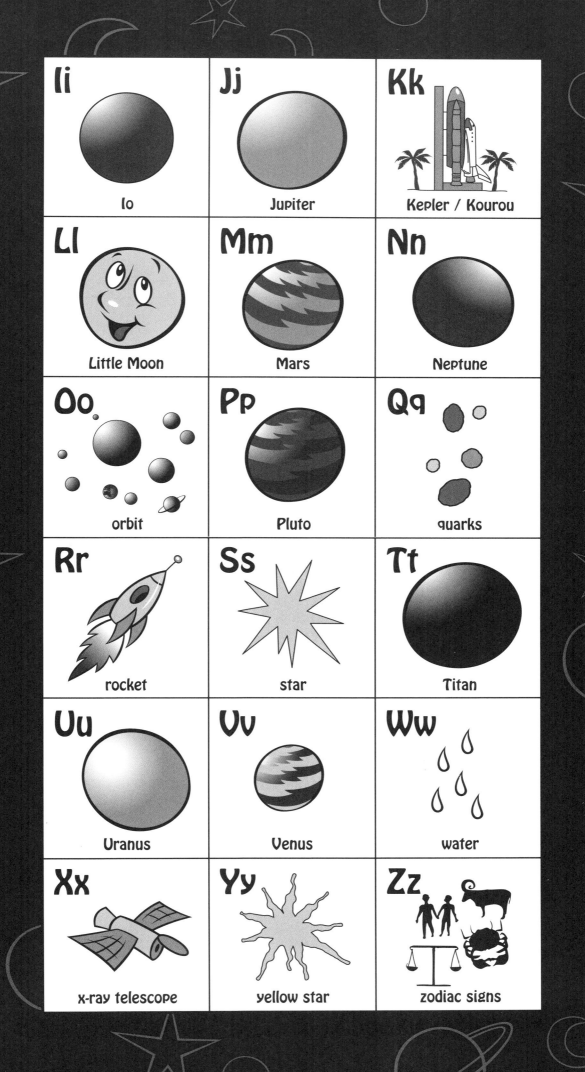

Hands Across the Universe!

Preparation and Resources:

Photocopy Activity Sheet Nos 16 and 17 for your own reference.
If seasonal, find a field with daisies.
Cut strips from coloured paper to make a paper chain.
Bring in a small collection of chains e.g. chain-link fence, necklace chain, etc.
You will need scissors.
Prepare sets of the chains for the children to cut out.

15cm 4cm

Opener:

Take the children into the hall or outside on to the playground.
Play 'chain tag'. If a child is tagged, they must join the chain.
Play singing games that involve the children holding hands, e.g. 'Ring a Ring O' Roses'.
Ask the whole class to join hands in a long chain.
Play 'follow my leader' but stay joined as a chain.
Collect daisies if it is seasonal.
Return to the classroom.
Show the children the collection of chains you have brought in.
Show them how to make a paper chain or daisy chain.
Make a paper chain to stretch across the classroom.

fine motor skills • singing

Useful questions to ask:

What is meant by joining? • Where do we see chains?
Why are chains used? • What is a chain?

Activity:

Using the images from Activity Sheet Nos 16 and 17, let the children create their own paper chains.

Step 1
Fold an A4 sheet in 4.

Step 2
Draw an alien or astronaut image on the front page. The hands must reach to the edge of the page both sides. This drawing can be done by an adult or child.

Step 3
Cut out the shape.

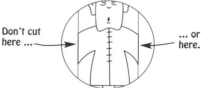

Don't cut here ... ... or here.

Age and stage of development will dictate if the child is able to cut out their own figure. Now join the children's chains with staples and stretch them across the classroom.

Extension:

More able pupils could design their own aliens or a chain could be made with people of different nationalities, creating a 'chain across the world.'

Vocabulary:

chain, link, join

fine motor skills • singing

ACTIVITY SHEET NO 16

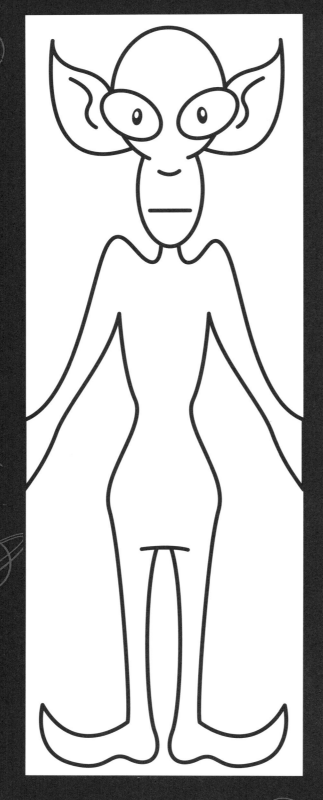 

fine motor skills • singing

ACTIVITY SHEET NO 17

fine motor skills • singing

Solar Sandwiches!

All children adore eating and making sandwiches, so why not have a sandwich party?

Here are a few suggestions to start the fun.

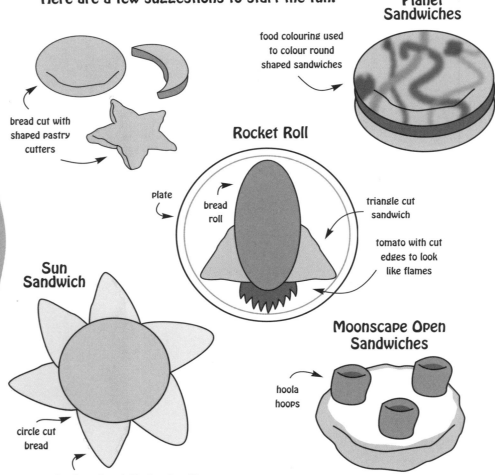

food technology • design & make

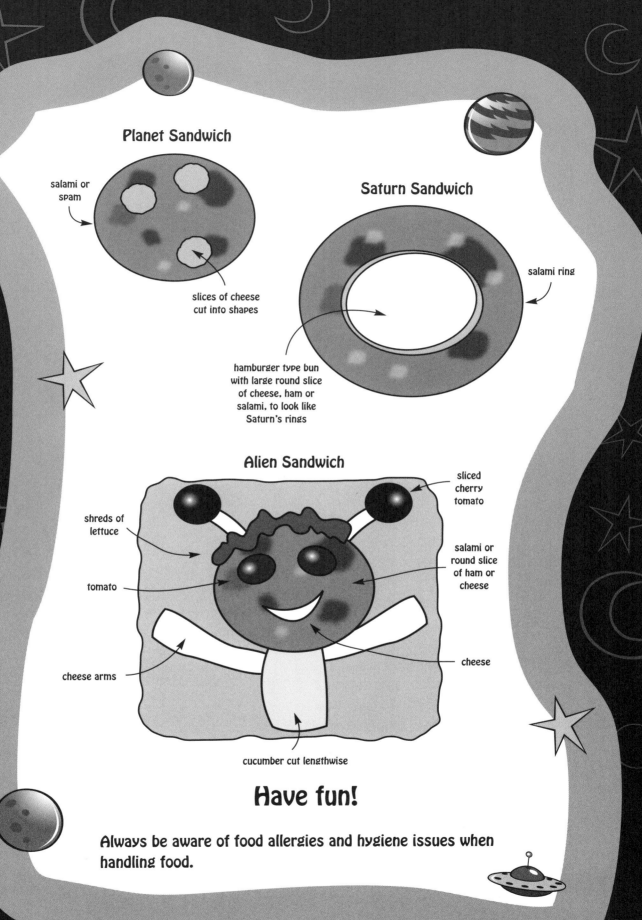

Little Moon's Word Search!

Look at the words from the story at the bottom of this page. They are hidden in the squares. Little Moon needs your help to find them. Draw a ring around each word when you find it. Try doing it with a friend.

P	Z	M	E	A	R	T	H
W	L	K	A	L	M	E	Y
C	S	U	O	R	F	P	X
N	J	Q	T	C	S	L	T
D	U	M	O	O	N	A	K
S	T	A	R	M	L	N	W
U	A	S	Z	E	B	E	A
N	I	G	P	T	X	T	H

SUN   COMET   MOON   MARS   EARTH
STAR   PLUTO   PLANET

letter recognition